SCIENCE OF FUN STUFF

The Cool Story Behind
Snow

PEACHTREE

by meteorologist Joe Rao
illustrated by Dagney Downey

Ready-to-Read

Simon Spotlight
New York   London   Toronto   Sydney   New Delhi

SIMON SPOTLIGHT
An imprint of Simon & Schuster Children's Publishing Division
1230 Avenue of the Americas, New York, New York 10020
This Simon Spotlight edition October 2015
Text copyright © 2015 by Simon & Schuster, Inc.
Illustrations copyright © 2015 by Dagney Downey
For information about special discounts for bulk purchases, please contact Simon & Schuster
Special Sales at 1-866-506-1949 or business@simonandschuster.com
The Simon & Schuster Speakers Bureau can bring authors to your live event. For more information or to book an
event contact the Simon & Schuster Speakers Bureau at 1-866-248-3049
or visit our website at www.simonspeakers.com.
Manufactured in the United States of America 0915 LAK
2 4 6 8 10 9 7 5 3 1
This book has been cataloged with the Library of Congress.
ISBN 978-1-4814-4413-2 (pbk)
ISBN 978-1-4814-4414-9 (hc)
ISBN 978-1-4814-4415-6 (eBook)

CONTENTS

Chapter 1: Water, Water, Everywhere   5

Chapter 2: Colliding Crystals   12

Chapter 3: Recipe for a Snowstorm   22

Chapter 4: Hail, Sleet, and Freezing Rain   30

But Wait . . . There's More!   41

CHAPTER 1
Water, Water, Everywhere

Has this ever happened to you? It's early on a winter's morning. You slowly open your eyes and look at your alarm clock. It's almost time to get ready for school.

Suddenly your mom comes into the bedroom. "You can stay in bed," she says. "There's no school today."

"Why?" you ask.

"Look out your window and you'll see for yourself," she says. You raise the window shade and see . . . snow! Everything is covered in a thick blanket of white. And more snow is falling hard and fast.

It's a snow day! Gazing out your window at this amazing wintry scene, you suddenly have a thought: Just what makes it snow?

To better understand what makes it snow, you first need to know that about three-quarters of the Earth's surface is covered by water. And the oceans hold almost all of Earth's water. Ninety-seven percent of Earth's water comes from the oceans, and is salt water. The other 3 percent is freshwater and is found in rivers, freshwater lakes, and swamps, as well as locked in frozen form within polar ice caps and glaciers.

Water is constantly evaporating from the oceans, rising into the atmosphere as vapor, and turning into very tiny water droplets that form clouds. This is part of the **water cycle**.

Any kind of water that falls from the sky (rain, sleet, ice, or snow) is called **precipitation** (pre-si-pe-tay-shun).

Every cloud is made up of water droplets, or if the temperature is below freezing, ice crystals.

The water droplets that form clouds are very tiny. How tiny?

Well, it takes about a *million* cloud droplets just to make one single raindrop! So it takes *billions* of droplets to form one cloud.

On their own, water droplets and dust particles simply float inside a cloud because they're so tiny and light. But when there are countless millions of them, the droplets collide with one another, clinging together and becoming bigger and heavier.

Eventually the cloud becomes too heavy, and gravity causes the water droplets to fall back to Earth as rain.

CHAPTER 2
Colliding Crystals

Now we know how we get raindrops. But how do we get snowflakes?

Floating high in our atmosphere are very tiny particles of dust. When the temperature inside a cloud falls below freezing, water vapor collects on these dust particles to form tiny ice crystals.

The shapes of the six "arms" of crystals form as water vapor freezes onto the ice crystals. These shapes can be plates, columns, and needles.

Now, remember how a raindrop forms? Countless numbers of tiny water droplets cling together to make a single raindrop.

Now imagine countless numbers of *ice crystals* colliding with water vapor, partially melting on contact and refreezing on their way down to the ground. In the end we get a snowflake, which always has six sides . . . the end result of countless crashes with other tiny shattered and melted ice crystals.

Why does a snowflake always have six sides? Well, the water molecules that make up an ice crystal are arranged in a special way so that they always form six-sided patterns called **hexagons**. As they fall to the ground, the various parts of a snowflake encounter slightly different temperatures and different amounts of water vapor, determining the shape that forms as the crystal grows. And because of this, no two snowflakes can ever be exactly alike!

Snowflakes in the Summer? Snow Way!

Have you ever been caught in a sudden summer shower or a thunderstorm?

If you have, remember that the clouds in sudden rainstorms can rise very high into the sky, sometimes over fifty thousand feet. The tops of these clouds are so cold they can contain a mixture of both ice crystals and **supercooled** water.

This supercooled water is made up of droplets of water that freeze quickly.

As the droplets fall through the cloud, ice crystals rapidly form snowflakes. But as these flakes reach the lower part of the cloud where the temperature is warmer, they melt and turn into rain.

So the next time you get caught in a drenching summer rainstorm, remember that the rain pouring on your head may have started out as snow! Of course, during the winter the air is cold enough for snowflakes to make it all the way down to the ground.

Fabulous Flakes!

Snowflakes are made of water. When the temperature is several degrees below freezing, you can get a lot of snow from just one inch of rain.

But this can change depending on other conditions. When it gets very cold, snow can become puffy and fluffy . . . almost a

fine powder, like sand or sugar. That's the kind of snow that doesn't make a good snowball or snowman. With puffy snow, you might get as much as twenty or even twenty-five inches of snow out of a single inch of rain!

But when the temperature is much milder and hovers within a degree or two of the freezing mark, snow tends to be slushier and mushier. These snowflakes become larger—the size of nickels and quarters. They are also much heavier and more difficult to push around with a shovel. Out of one inch of rain, you might get only about five inches of soggy, wet snow.

Why do lower temperatures create lighter, fluffier snow? The surrounding air can't hold as much moisture when it is cold. This means that at 32°F, air can hold more water than when it is colder out. So snowflakes are larger and heavier because they contain more water. At colder temperatures the snow contains less water and the flakes are smaller, puffier, and lighter.

So what's the best weather for building a snowman? Somewhere in between the two extremes! The temperature should be a bit below freezing, but not too cold or else it will turn out to be the puffy "sugar snow."

Riddle: What do you call an old snowman?

Answer: Water!

CHAPTER 3
Recipe for a Snowstorm

We all want a snow day! So, how do we make a snowstorm?

The first ingredient in this "recipe" must be cold air. In order to have a snowstorm the air must be at or below freezing, from the cloud tops down to the ground. During the winter, cold air from Canada is pushed south into the United States by strong winds in the upper part of the atmosphere, known as the **jet stream**.

The next ingredient is a flow of warm, moist air to create clouds and precipitation. That moisture usually comes from the Gulf of Mexico. You've learned rain and snowflakes form from colliding water drops and ice crystals. Well, a snowstorm occurs from colliding warm and cold air. Because warm moist air is lighter than cold dry air, the warm air rises above the cold air, forming a boundary zone called a **front**.

If you've ever watched the weather forecast on TV, you've probably seen the weather map showing different kinds of fronts.

The leading edge of a push of cold dry air is called a **cold front**, while the leading edge of a push of warm moist air is a **warm front**.

When the cold dry air and the warm moist air reach a standoff and don't move very much, the boundary zone between them is called a **stationary front**.

Winter storms will usually form along a stationary front when the front bends or wavers. The air will begin to move in a counterclockwise direction, forming a storm system.

Just how strong a storm will get depends on how much moisture and energy is available. In some cases, the storm may become very strong, producing strong winds and heavy snow.

Blizzards

You've probably heard people say, "It's a blizzard out there!" during a snowstorm. Not all snowstorms are blizzards, though. When the winds are blowing constantly at speeds of thirty-five miles per hour or more and snow is falling heavily, then we call that a blizzard. Blizzards are dangerous because the combination of falling and blowing snow can make it hard to see. When you can see for only a short distance ahead of you, it's called **whiteout** conditions.

The best place to be during a blizzard is indoors! You should never try to travel or go outside when a blizzard is raging.

CHAPTER 4
Hail, Sleet, and Freezing Rain

Frozen precipitation can come in more forms than just snow.

During the spring and summer months, hail can fall. Hail starts out as a frozen raindrop, which gets tossed up and down inside a cloud by strong winds during a thunderstorm.

Collisions with other raindrops, followed by freezing and refreezing, causes layers of ice to form. When it finally gets too heavy, it falls to the ground as hail.

Hail most often is the size of a pea or marble. But some hailstones can grow to be much larger—as large as a golf ball, or even a softball.

SIZES OF HAILSTONES

PEA SIZE   GOLF BALL SIZE   SOFTBALL SIZE

If you cut a hailstone in half, you'll see rings of clear and cloudy ice, indicating the number of times it got tossed up and down in a thunderstorm cloud.

Sometimes during the winter a layer of warm air develops in the upper part of the atmosphere and precipitation falls as rain.

Closer to the ground, however, the temperature is at or below freezing.

The raindrops freeze just before hitting the ground, falling as ice pellets called **sleet**, which can bounce upon hitting the ground. Sleet makes driving dangerous, so if you must travel when it's icy, remember to always "fasten your *sleet (seat) belt!*" if you see these ice pellets falling.

Ice storms are caused by freezing rain. Freezing rain is different from sleet in that it falls like ordinary rain until it hits any solid object that is at or below freezing. The rain then freezes on contact with the object, which soon becomes covered by a thin layer of ice, which is called a **glaze**.

Because streets and roadways are usually dark in color, and because the icy glaze is clear and difficult to see, it's sometimes called **black ice**. People driving cars may not see this ice and skid on the road. This is why ice on streets and roads is extremely dangerous to drivers.

When freezing rain falls for a long time, thick layers of ice can pile up on trees and power lines and cause lots of damage. Ice storms can be beautiful, but also very destructive!

Riddle: How does a snowman get to work?
Answer: By icicle!

THE LAKE-EFFECT SNOW...

VERY COLD AIR

MILD AIR

WARM LAKE WATER

Sometimes it's not a storm that can bring heavy snow, but the wind. When very cold air blows over large bodies of relatively mild water like the Great Lakes, it can pick up lots of water vapor, which then freezes into snow and quickly piles up near the shores of lakes that face into the wind. This type of "wind over water" snow (also known as **lake-effect snow**) can produce blizzard conditions and drop a huge amount of snow in a very short time.

Sometimes thunder and lightning
will occur during a snowstorm—
"thundersnow!"

This can happen when the atmosphere
becomes very **turbulent**—rough, stormy,
and unstable—and the air is rapidly forced
upward through the clouds.

The effect is similar to a thunderstorm
in the summertime, except instead of a
downpour, you can get a burst of very
heavy snowfall that can drop several
inches of snow or more in a single hour!

37

In the United States large amounts of snow can be found in several different places. Lots of snow falls in parts of the Northeast and around the Great Lakes, as well as out west in the Rocky Mountains.

The least amount of snow falls in Florida and along the Gulf coasts of Texas and Louisiana. In these parts of the country, it's too warm to snow for most of the year.

As a result, snowfall for these places averages only one-tenth of one inch each winter, and very often there are winters where no snow falls at all.

But snow has fallen in all fifty states. It can even snow in Hawaii, though this can happen only in places that are very high up. It might be 80°F on a beach in Honolulu, while at the same time the tops of Hawaii's highest volcanoes are getting dusted with snow!

SCIENCE OF FUN STUFF EXPERT ON SNOW

Congratulations! You've come to the end of this book. You are now an official Science of Fun Stuff Expert on snow. So the next time you're home enjoying a snow day, remember the science behind the fun!

Hey, kids! Now that you're an expert on the science of snow, turn the page to learn even more about weather and some weather-predicting tools along the way!

Weather by the Numbers

Biggest Snowflake

On January 28, 1887, at Fort Keough, Montana, snowflakes as large as fifteen inches were seen falling from the sky and splattering to the ground! (That's bigger than the spread across these two pages!)

Biggest Hailstone

The biggest hailstone on record fell in Vivian, South Dakota, in 2010. Even after melting a bit, the stone weighed nearly two pounds, with a **circumference** (the distance around the stone) of 18.62 inches.

The Snowiest Place in America

The snowiest place in the United States is Mount Rainier in Washington state. It snows there about 121 days a year and totals an average of 643 inches. That's almost fifty-four *feet* of snow!

Coldest Place on Earth

The coldest place on Earth is on the East Antarctic Plateau in Antarctica, where temperatures can dip below -128.5°F.

Many people think the North Pole is the coldest place on Earth, but this is wrong. The North Pole is much warmer than the South Pole because it lies at sea level in the middle of an ocean, which acts as a supply source of heat. The South Pole lies within a landmass (Antarctica) at an elevation of 9,000 feet (1.76 miles up.)

Rainiest Place on Earth

The village of Mawsynram in northeast India is considered the wettest place in the world. The village receives about 467 inches of rain per year. In order to protect themselves as they work in the fields, villagers wear turtlelike-shell coverings on their bodies when it rains.

How Does a Meteorologist Predict the Weather?

Each day weather forecasts are made by **meteorologists**, scientists who study and predict the weather. They rely on sophisticated equipment to help them with their forecasts. Equipment like:

Doppler Radar

In 1842, Austrian scientist Christian Doppler came up with an idea known as "the Doppler effect." He noticed that sound waves have a higher frequency as the sound source moves toward the observer and a lower frequency as the source moves away from the observer. Next time you hear an ice-cream truck, listen closely: The song it plays will sound higher as it approaches you, but it'll sound lower as it drives away!

Weather radars send out radio waves from an antenna. Doppler radars measure the frequency change in returning radio waves. Like the music from the ice-cream truck, radio waves moving away from the antenna change to a lower frequency, and waves moving toward it change to a higher frequency. The frequency changes tell meteorologists the direction and speeds of wind, helping them to predict what's going to happen weather-wise.

Satellite Photographs

Satellite photos help meteorologists by tracking the path of upcoming storms. Weather satellites are orbiting the Earth all the time—some are as high as twenty-two thousand miles above the ground! They give meteorologists information about what is happening in places where there are no weather stations to take readings.

Research Planes

In the United States there are several different types of Hurricane Hunter aircraft, which are used to monitor hurricanes. Some of these planes are built to fly right into the eye of the storm. The planes are usually designed with extra-long "noses" that hold instrument panels. The panels detect wind speed and direction, temperature, humidity, and other information about a storm.

Weather Balloons

Everyone loves balloons, but it may surprise you that balloons are some of a meteorologist's most important weather tools! Every day weather balloons are launched from 102 sites across the United States, Caribbean, and Pacific.

Each balloon is attached to an instrument called a **radiosonde**. As the balloon rises, the radiosonde measures conditions in the atmosphere, such as air pressure, temperature, and humidity. The radiosonde takes readings at various heights, from the ground to nearly twenty miles in the air. This information is then relayed to ground stations, where computers use the information to forecast the state of the atmosphere.

With all the fancy technology available today, why are balloons the best way to get information? Rockets would zoom through the atmosphere too quickly. Jet planes usually stay in just one layer of the atmosphere. The best way to get a complete

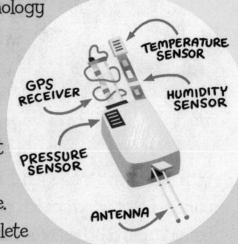

GPS RECEIVER

TEMPERATURE SENSOR

HUMIDITY SENSOR

PRESSURE SENSOR

ANTENNA

reading of all the layers of the atmosphere in a specific place and time is to use something that rises slowly. For this purpose, balloons are the perfect weather instrument!

After the weather balloon reaches an altitude of about a hundred thousand feet, it will burst. (If the balloon bursts earlier than planned due to exceptionally cold conditions, a replacement balloon is launched, probably made with a heavier-duty type of rubber to prevent this from happening again.) When the balloon bursts, a small parachute on the radiosonde pops open and the radiosonde falls gently back to Earth. Radiosondes have landed in trees, on bridges, and even in people's backyards! The radiosonde lands with its own addressed, postage-paid return mailbag so that whoever finds it can mail it back to the National Weather Service. The radiosondes are then recycled and prepared for another launch.

Being an expert on something means you can get an
awesome score on a quiz on that subject! Take this

SCIENCE OF SNOW QUIZ

to see how much you've learned.

1. Any water that falls from the sky is called?

a. sleet   b. precipitation   c. rain

2. Raindrops are formed by

a. colliding water droplets   b. colliding ice crystals   c. frozen water

3. A snowflake always has

a. rounded edges   b. a triangular center   c. six sides

4. Cold and warm air colliding is a good start for a possible

a. rainy day   b. snowstorm   c. rainbow

5. When the temperature lingers around the freezing mark, any snow that falls will
   probably be

a. heavy and slushy   b. light and fluffy   c. perfect for building a
                                                       snowman

6. Strong winds in the upper part of the atmosphere are known as

a. gusts   b. fronts   c. the jet stream

7. If you cut a hailstone in half, the rings inside will tell you

a. the temperature   b. how many inches   c. how many times it was
                                                       tossed in a thundercloud

8. Water vapor on dust particles creates ice crystals, which, when temperatures
   drop, turn into

a. snowflakes   b. black ice   c. sleet

Answers: 1. b 2. a 3. c 4. b 5. a 6. c 7. c 8. a